LIFE IS *Decisions*

STEPHEN PERRY

Life is Decisions
Copyright © 2018 Stephen Perry

ISBN: 978-1-5136-3456-2

CONTENTS

DEDICATION

As I look back over my life, from as far back as I can remember, it's evident to me that God had a call on my life. He orchestrated things to get me to places where my destiny would be protected. That started with me being raised by my grandparents. Although they never told me, I believe they knew that raising me was more than just raising a child; it was protecting a calling from God.

This book is dedicated to my grandmother and grandfather, the late Reverend Richard Gates and the late Mrs. Lizzie Gates. I thank God that you guys put up with me, loved me and protected me—both physically and spiritually. I love and miss you both so much. I'll see you both soon after my mission here on earth is done.

ACKNOWLEDGMENTS

First and foremost, I would like to thank my Heavenly Father and my Lord and Savior Jesus Christ. Without God's grace and mercy, I wouldn't be here. I would like to give a special thanks to my wife for always being by my side, especially when I was going through the issues pertaining to my kidney transplant. I would like to thank my kids who are and will always be dear to me.

I would like to extend a special thanks to all of the following people, who in one way or another, have had a great impact on my life: my grandparents, Richard Gates and Lizzie Gates; my sweet mother, Linda Carr; my uncles: the late Reverend Harvie Gates and Robert Gates; my aunts: Lois January, Christine Pruiett, Ann Harris, and Mary Thomas ; my cousins: Joyce Gates, Natalie Thomas, Sheila Blaze, and Darrin Farmer.

I love all of you, and I am forever grateful to each and every one of you for the impact you've made in my life.

INTRODUCTION

Back in the late 90s after recognizing and finally accepting the call of God on my life to the gospel ministry, I began to also realize that God had given me a special gift—an ability to understand things pertaining to life and an ability to explain these things plainly. A few years ago, God gave me an overall definition of life from the human perspective. He said, "Life is nothing more than a series of decisions." And as I began to evaluate this statement, I found it to be nothing short of the truth—100%. Everything we do, have ever done, and will ever do—even if influenced by others in some form—is because of the decisions we make, have made, or will make. The quality of life we have today was strongly influenced by the day to day decisions we've made in the past. Therefore, our ability to make good or righteous decisions (according to the righteousness of God) is vital.

This book consists of a series of proverbs that will provide inspiration for making better decisions. A proverb is a short saying stating a general truth or piece of advice. From proverbs, we gain exposure to certain truths that we might not have known, or we gain a deeper understanding of those truths which will enable us to become good decision makers. We have everything we need in the Book of Proverbs in the Bible, so by no means am I adding to the Bible or suggesting I know something that needs to be added. But rather I'm giving you a modern-day version of what has already been written, exactly as the Lord gave it to me in the midst of my ups and downs and everyday struggles, so you can draw wisdom from them and hopefully be inspired to become good or better decision makers.

CHAPTER 1
Pure Faith Language

*W*hen it comes to having a relationship with God and man, faith is what makes and sustains that connection. It is faith that enables us to become God's children and live the way God wants us to live. In one of Paul's letters to the Church at Corinth, he said that Christians are to live by faith (Romans 10). In order to live by faith, one of the things we must understand is the importance of what we speak.

Paul also wrote in Romans chapter 10 that salvation is obtained through the combination of belief and confession. It is no different with the rest of our walk with Christ. Our belief and confession brings manifestation. With this being true, we must train ourselves to speak a pure faith language as opposed to speaking what our feelings would move us to speak. In other words, we speak what we believe and once we speak it, we give legs and feet to it.

What is Faith

1. Faith is what connects men to God.

2. Faith is the bridge that makes God and man's relationship work.

3. Living by faith is having the ability to resist what we feel and stand on what God said.

4. The God kind-of-faith and trusting in God go together.

5. Pure faith makes impossibilities nonexistent.

6. True faith loves God.

7. True faith breeds true followers.

8. Faith enabled the saints of old to speak loudly today.

9. True faith doesn't allow fear to stop it.

10. Faith dispels deception.

11. True faith comes down to being faithful an obedient.

12. Faith is the evidence of the thing you're believing God for.

13. True faith speaks of things to come and lives as if it has already happened.

14. We are what we believe.

15. Whatever you truly believe is bearing fruit in your life right now.

16. Faith requires patience, therefore, we must master the art of waiting.

17. In order to receive God's best, you must first truly believe in God.

18. If you're willing to take the first step, God will assist you in making the next one.

19. Only faith in Jesus leads to eternal life.

20. Faith is resilient; it never gives up.

21. True faith enables us to have the patience and endurance necessary to win.

22. Faith doesn't wonder, it knows.

23. Ask and believe. Provision has already been made for what we need.

24. The things we can see only last for a little while, but the things we can't see last forever. This is why faith is so important.

25. Genuine faith is not having to have physical proof in order to believe.

26. Faith is the bridge between the seen and unseen worlds.

27. The reason why we are commanded to live by faith and not by sight is because faith is spiritual sight, revealing the things we can't see naturally.

Growing in Faith

1. The truth has to be exposed before faith can come.

2. Just as the sun rises before the day is fully come, so it is with the truth, meaning truth has to be understood before faith can manifest.

3. Because of the fact that every human being is created in God's image, we were born with all the faith we will ever need inside of us.

4. Because of adverse circumstances and/or false teachings, the faith we have has to be polished through the Word of God in order to become pure.

5. The more we get to know God, the more polished and genuine our faith becomes.

6. Faith enables ordinary men to do extraordinary things.

7. Faith gives us access into God's kingdom.

8. Faith gives us access to God's peace.

9. True freedom comes and is sustained in your life when you begin to believe and confess this: "Lord, not my will but yours be done."

10. True courage doesn't allow fear to stop it.

11. Although there are many struggles in life, nothing is too hard for those who walk with the Lord.

12. If we speak the Word and have faith that it's true, it works.

13. Believers are called to live by faith every day until it becomes natural, not to try it and tap in only when trouble comes.

14. Real faith acts upon what it says it believes.

15. God's perspective on faith is to trust Him, meaning have enough faith to do what He says even if there is some doubt lingering.

16. It's impossible to please God without faith, so you gotta have it.

17. Faith requires that we deny our flesh and trust God's word.

18. Some people have the gift of faith, meaning God anointed them with a gift to be able to believe even in adverse circumstances.

19. Your faith isn't genuine if your confession and actions don't match.

20. Just as a warrior conquers kingdoms, in the same way faith conquers impossibilities.

21. True faith isn't phased by false teaching. It stands strong on the Word of God.

22. Faith stops any momentum that the enemy has against you.

23. Pure faith can overcome selfishness.

Those Who Believe

1. Faith makes the realm of heaven visible on earth.

2. It's by faith that we discover who we are, and it is faith that enables us to manifest what we discover.

3. In order to believe in God, you must believe in Jesus.

4. Faith connected to the core of our being produces real seeing.

5. You're unstoppable when you bring your faith to the fight.

6. True faith sees the outcome of a situation no matter how bad things get.

7. God is mighty and God is great. God draws nigh and responds to pure faith.

8. True faith consists of a combination or belief and doing. Belief alone is not faith.

9. In order for true faith to be complete, an act has to be attached to your belief.

10. True faith produces those that are faithful and those that are faithful will be rewarded.

11. Sincere faith absolutely gets God excited!

12. True faith can't be still or silent; it is compelled to take action.

13. Nothing that life can throw at a faith-filled person can stop them.

14. It's very difficult to deceive pure faith.

15. Circumstances have no bearing on pure faith. It believes its way through them all.

16. God desires to be in control of our lives. Faith gives Him permission to do so.

Faith Seals the Deal

1. When it comes to what God said, there are no buts.

2. Faith triumphs over troubles.

3. The moment you decide to believe for a thing, without doubting, it becomes real.

4. The combination of believing and speaking what you believe establishes that thing as reality and sets the course in motion for it to manifest.

5. What we see is really an illusion. It's what we can't see that is real.

6. We discover who we are and manifest these truths by faith.

7. Faith in Jesus is what seals our redemption.

8. Everything and everybody that exists, with the exception of God Himself, came to be by faith.

9. No matter how good we think we are or how many good things we do, God only responds to our faith.

10. Even though the spiritual experiences you may have aren't nearly as many as the fleshy experiences you have, the spiritual experiences are still what is true. Don't let the flesh dictate reality to you.

11. God is faithful. Whatever He called you to do, He will provide everything necessary to make it happen. Trust Him.

12. Faith and confidence in the authority God has given you is the distance between you and the manifestation of what you ask God for, according to His will.

13. If you truly believe in God, you are willing to put what He says above any desires you have that contradicts what He said.

14. Although the Bible is full of promises relating to believers, believers will only benefit from the ones that they truly believe.

15. Faith in Jesus makes us righteous.

16. Faith makes things you can't see just as real as the things you can see.

17. True faith is having the patience to stand and wait on God, knowing He's going to do what He said no matter what's going on.

18. Faith transitions from temporary to eternal.

19. Faith moves us from powerless to powerful.

20. Faith moves us from hopelessness to victory.

21. The reason why Jesus was in so much agony in the Garden of Gethsemane was because He was to experience a disconnect from the Father for the first time ever on the cross. At that point, it was His faith that enabled Him to finish His mission.

22. Pure faith equals pure power.

23. When fear steps in the ring with faith, faith is the undisputed champion.

24. It has been recorded in the scriptures that pure faith can even cause God to change His mind.

This Isn't Faith

1. Faith can't operate in a doubt-filled environment.

2. Don't accept a contrary report when God already spoke on the matter.

3. We won't experience the power of God in our lives if we don't truly have faith in God.

4. Faith focuses on the outcome of a situation. It doesn't focus on how things seem at the time.

5. Our feelings are faith killers! Don't trust them.

6. Faith doesn't give up when tribulations come. It stands even stronger.

7. Where there is a lack of commitment, there is a lack of faith.

8. Some people don't believe in God because they can't see Him, yet they believe in other things that they can't see daily.

9. Without faith in God, disaster awaits you.

10. Sometimes disobedience is due to a lack of faith.

CHAPTER 2
Wisdom for Every day

*W*isdom, from God's point of view, is having the ability to take knowledge or understanding and make righteous decisions with it (according to God's righteousness). As we go through life, we are faced with making decisions all day, every single day. Having Godly knowledge and wisdom is key to being equipped to make decisions that are going to please God and prosper us as opposed to bringing eventual destruction in our lives.

According to Psalms 147:5, God's understanding is limitless, therefore, if He is the source of our decision making, by obtaining His knowledge and wisdom, our lives will be rewarded greatly. Remember, *life is decisions*!

Wisdom for Righteous Living

1. True wisdom starts with having great respect for the Lord.

2. True wisdom begins when your respect and adoration for the Lord becomes genuine.

3. Strongholds can be broken, but we must allow the Holy Spirit to teach us how to break them. Each situation is different.

4. We can't do enough living to catch up with what is already recorded in the Word. It's alive.

5. A lot of people can't understand truth, especially in the form of correction because they're looking at the information through lenses of selfishness.

6. Sometimes it's best to answer foolishness without answering the initial question. Instead, answer with a statement that gets to the root of the matter.

7. God wants and deserves all of our heart. Playing both sides of the fence is worse than choosing a sinful lifestyle.

8. Whatever kind of company you keep, you will eventually become.

9. If we fail to learn the basics of Christianity, our walk will always be feeble.

10. When praying for people to come to or grow in Christ, the focus must not be on the progress or lack thereof with the person, but rather trusting in God.

11. An unwillingness to be humble breeds spiritual blindness.

12. Jesus was able to do what He did because He was filled with the Spirit. Likewise, in order for us to do God's will, we must also be filled with the Spirit of God.

13. Our job is not to figure out how God does what He says, but rather to believe He can and will do it.

14. Pride brings destruction, but God honors humbleness.

15. Marriage in a nutshell boils down to two people (husband and wife) becoming one. Marriage is about oneness.

16. Marriage is instituted by sexual relations, but it is consummated by taking vows with one another before the Lord.

17. You can give all you want, but God is only pleased with the portion that you gave sincerely.

18. From day-to-day situations in the life of an individual, all the way up to the behavior of an entire nation, when God is absent, chaos reigns.

19. Jesus didn't die because He didn't have anything better to do. He died because we were in eternal jeopardy.

20. Going to church doesn't necessarily mean you know God.

21. If God and His ways don't dominate your thought-life, something or someone else is taking His place.

22. Giving our lives to God is a life of servanthood, not an escape from trouble.

Making Righteous Decisions

1. Brokenness that is kept hidden can never be healed. Instead, it subtly leads to total destruction.

2. Sometimes separation is necessary before true unity can happen. In other words, sometimes you have to separate in order to come together.

3. If you truly believe in God, you are willing to put what He says above any desires you have that contradicts what He said.

4. Living apart from God is no different than committing suicide.

5. Even though some things are permissible, if they are not done from a sincere heart, God is not pleased.

6. One of the most powerful decisions you can make in life is to have a made-up mind about accepting Christ.

7. Doing the right thing at the wrong time can prove to be costly.

8. Whatever you allow into your heart will shape your outlook on life and drastically impact your decisions and lifestyle, so be careful of what you watch and listen to.

9. Whatever lifestyle you adopt, there is a god attached to it.

10. Many people may claim to be friends, but only those that remain loyal are true friends.

11. When we've gone through trials we can either suffer and reap a blessing, or we can suffer twice.

12. Before we set out to make moves in our lives, it's wise that we have heard from God who is going to show us the big picture first. This way you know what you're striving to do and not just throwing darts in the dark.

13. Life will bring storms and our willingness to accept and go through the storm, so to speak, will ultimately determine our victory in the situation.

14. Never judge a person by what someone else said about them. Get to know them for yourself and then judge accordingly.

15. Only those who truly reverence the Lord are wise.

16. Being a real man or woman is knowing how to make right decisions and being disciplined enough to make them.

17. The source of our motivation determines our outlook on a matter.

18. Some people hate others because they are of different ethnicities, yet they are dependent upon these same people in one way or another.

19. Truth is not based on how we feel.

20. Some of what we consider to be love is really harmful tolerance.

Wisdom for Personal Growth

1. Sometimes we have to grow into the things we learn. In some cases, it can be things that came out of our own mouths.

2. Just because something is not wrong in and of itself doesn't mean it's not wrong for you, especially if it can become excessive or addictive.

3. The closer you are to a person, the harder it is to resist being in your feelings.

4. When our personal experiences (trials, struggles, surroundings, etc.) become our reality, we've entered into a danger zone because reality at this point is one-sidedly lacking the perspective of the whole picture.

5. Just like Jesus is the only way to heaven, Jesus is also the only way to discovering you.

6. Some people are so sensitive that they would rather hear a lie as opposed to the truth. Learn to accept the truth and be healed.

7. Some messages are hard yet simple—hard because of our perception, simple because a change of perception takes place removing the hard.

8. Never despise growing older. With age comes experience, maturity, and wisdom.

9. As long as we live, we should be growing in Christ.

10. You are a product of what your heart contains.

11. We can only have what God promises when we believe what He says.

12. In order for growth to take place, some type of change is necessary.

13. Your decision-making stems from what is most important to you.

14. There comes a time when you have to stop just coping with your situation and deal with it.

15. It's good to be passionate, but be careful and don't allow the devil to use it against you.

16. God doesn't base success on numbers or anything physical, but rather on obedience and faithfulness. Keep pressing forward.

17. God's promises are made void by our lack of faith.

18. We are very limited when we decide to follow our own way, but when we submit our lives to God, our possibilities are limitless.

19. A wise man once said that the wisdom of youth will never surpass the wisdom of their elders.

20. Just because we tune God out, doesn't mean He doesn't see everything we do.

21. As Christians, no matter how many times we mess up, we are called to repent, keep moving forward, and instill God's standards on earth.

22. No one is perfect, but in Christ, perfection should become a progressive goal.

23. Judas still exists today. Even though it was a part of Jesus' destiny to keep him around, that doesn't mean *we* are supposed to.

Knowledge for Every Day

1. While on a quest to expose the oppression of the enemy, make sure not to become the enemy.

2. Being ignorant causes lack, but being ignorant of your ignorance is tragic.

3. The things of the heart sometimes run so deep that words can't express them.

4. Nonverbal communication speaks way more truth than the tongue.

5. What you might consider being a burden might be an absolute dream come true to the next person. Count your blessings.

6. As witnesses, sometimes we must understand that some people have lived wrong for so long that wrong is right to them.

7. The foundation of all civilization is the family.

8. All wisdom is not profitable. Only the wisdom that comes from God is perfect.

9. Watch people and listen to what they say, and sooner or later they will show you who they really are.

10. If the devil can't trick and deceive you, his next move is to distract you.

11. Life is not fair, so trouble will come. Don't be alarmed or allow it to overtake you. Trust God and He will see you through.

12. If you're not willing to listen to wise instructions, you're headed for disaster by choice.

13. You can claim to be this and that, but your loyalty will be where your heart is.

14. Anyone that despises truth is wicked at heart.

15. If a person doesn't truly want change, change will never come.

16. Paths of Righteousness might not always refer to places where righteousness is going on.

17. When leaders make bad decisions, the whole team or organization suffers.

18. It's wise to deal with people for who they are, not necessarily for who they say they are.

19. Where there is a lack of confidence, self-esteem, or even extreme shyness lies an abundance of fear! But God didn't give us a spirit of fear, my friends, so take Him at His word and walk thereby.

20. Success has a direct tie to favor from God and men, but a spirit of disrespect kills any chances of having it.

21. Our lifestyles become the top priority in our lives. Whether good or bad, it produces the harvest we now live by.

22. Worldly wisdom doesn't teach us how to live a successful and fulfilling life.

23. When you choose to reject Christ, the knowledge you think you have is really rooted in the serpent.

24. God does things at His appointed time, not a moment later, not a moment earlier.

25. Sometimes we already have what we think we want. Don't let Satan trick and rob you.

26. God doesn't show favoritism.

27. Some people don't care about being right but would rather have their wrongdoing validated.

CHAPTER 3
Proverbs of Praise

*P*raise is one of the most powerful weapons we have in our spiritual arsenal, yet it is often not viewed as a weapon and is underutilized. Praise is simply any act committed or anything said that would bring glory to God. "Proverbs of Praise" is meant to help us understand the power of praise and help us develop a system and habit of speaking these things so that they eventually become a part of who we are.

At the end of the day, making it a habit to continuously praise God will turn us into true praisers, which is God's will for the lives of all of His children.

Why God Should be Praised

1. God should be praised simply because of who He is!

2. Praise shouldn't be hard when the person to whom it's due is perfect.

3. Although God should be praised overall simply for who He is, three things He should specifically be praised for are: His goodness, His mercy, and His love.

4. God should be praised for His worthiness.

5. God should be praised for His blessings.

6. God should be praised for being our comforter.

7. God should be praised for being our deliverer from bondage.

8. God should be praised for His forgiveness.

9. God should be praised for His grace.

10. God should be praised for His guidance. No other counsel can match the counsel of the Lord.

11. God should be praised for His promises and the fact that He keeps every one of them.

12. God should be praised for His love for He is love.

13. God should be praised for His salvation. Without His Son becoming a-once-and-for-all sacrifice, no one would be saved.

14. God should be praised for redemption.

15. God should be praised for His wisdom, which He is eager to give to His children whom ask.

16. God should be praised for the authority He has given to His children.

17. God should be praised for His glory and majesty. There's nothing or no one like our God.

18. God should be praised for His word for it is true. It is alive and full of power.

19. God should be praised for His strength, for He is Sovereign, the Almighty God.

20. God should be praised for His name, for His name is great.

21. The skies announce what God's hands have made and what He has done.

22. The grass speaks, the flowers yell, the trees and mountains utter His praise!

23. The sun and moon testify to His greatness continually.

24. There are an uncountable amount of reasons why God should be praised.

25. God should be praised because He is the giver of all life.

26. There is no deeper love than God's love. No one can love you like He does.

27. God should be praised for the great things He does.

28. God should be praised because He commands it, and because it pleases Him.

29. God should be praised for His greatness.

30. God should be praised for His grace and mercy.

31. God should be praised for His love and compassion.

32. God should be praised for glory and majesty.

33. God should be praised because He is our eternal Heavenly Father.

34. We should praise God for revealing His will.

35. God should be praised for the covenant He made with men and the fact that He keeps it.

36. God houses Himself in the midst of the praises of His people.

37. God's worthiness of being praised far exceeds our willingness or ability to praise Him.

38. Every moment we live is an opportunity to give God the praise that He's due.

39. God should be praised for His patience and long-suffering concerning us.

40. A perfect God deserves our most sincere praise.

41. We don't have the time or the capacity to truly give God the praise He is worthy of, but we can and should give Him all the praise, all the time, for all that He does.

42. God is glorified when His people praise Him.

43. God is pleased when His people praise Him.

44. We praise God for who He is, not for what we want from Him.

45. Even God's enemies owe Him praise because He loves them regardless.

What Praise Is

1. Praise should transition from accolades to real-life situations so that genuine praise comes forth.

2. True praise is not manufactured, it comes from the soul.

3. God wants our praise to become a lifestyle, not just singular acts here and there.

4. Giving thanks to God is one of the most important forms of praise.

5. Don't take thanksgiving for granted. It is a powerful weapon. God is praised when we thank Him for what He does or who He is.

6. Although praise is something that has to come from our hearts sincerely, God has to enable us to be in the position to sincerely give it.

7. Praise God, saints, by professing the name of Jesus.

8. Praise God, saints, by dancing before Him.

9. Praise God, saints, with service above and beyond your comfort zone.

10. Praise God, saints, with musical instruments.

11. Praise God, saints, by singing songs and hymns.

12. Pain creates the purest praise.

13. Praise, at some point, should become a lifestyle.

14. Like a mother gives birth to her child, so it is with praise and worship.

15. Worship is a continuous series of acts of praise.

16. Even though God commands us to praise Him, He only accepts it when it is pure and voluntary.

17. If we practice giving God praise at all times, in every situation, it will eventually become an automatic reaction.

18. Real encounters with God are moments that are very special and moments we'll never forget. This demonstrates the power of praise.

19. God wants us to live out our praise by doing whatever He gifted us to do for His glory.

20. A thankful heart praises God at all times in all things.

21. God is praised every time we utter that majestic name of Jesus.

22. Praise is birthed out of love while dressed in appreciation.

23. Praising God captions the reason for human existence.

24. Praise is our offense and defense in battle. Use it.

25. God should be praised with our entire being, from our thought life to our deeds.

26. True praise is when you're compelled to be obedient when you really don't want to be.

27. Our voluntary praise must still be accompanied by the power of the Holy Spirit.

28. God not only desire, but also commands to have the whole heart of His followers.

29. If we really appreciate God for who He is, praise comes naturally.

30. Just as God's love for us is unconditional, so should our praise be for Him.

31. Make praising God your lifestyle, not just random acts at church.

32. Praise is an outward expression of the depths of our love for God.

The Benefits of Praise

1. God wants intimacy with us. Lord, lead me to those places you have ordained for me to praise you.

2. Learn to praise God in your prayers.

3. Praising God in your prayers helps to produce a powerful prayer life.

4. Wherever saints come together to praise God is God's house.

5. Praise causes an immediate response from God through a manifestation of His presence.

6. True praise is more powerful than tanks, guns, and swords.

7. Speaking or calling on the name of Jesus brings glory to God.

8. Praise is just as much of a weapon as the Word in warfare.

9. When God moves in our lives, our response should be heartfelt praise.

10. One thing that causes God to move immediately is heartfelt praise.

11. Praise creates an inviting atmosphere for God to move freely.

12. Deliverance can come through sincere praise.

13. Praise momentarily brings heaven to earth.

14. Praise is personified when we put God first in everything.

15. When God is sincerely praised, people and places are affected.

16. God's chariot rides upon the praises of His people.

17. Praise draws us closer to God, and enables us to know Him on a deeper level.

18. When we praise God, we are attacking the enemy, and invading his camp.

19. Praising God ignites His favor.

20. Praise is in the arsenal of a warrior.

21. You wanna know how to get rid of depression? Start praising God!

22. Instead of hanging horse shoes over your front door to repel evil spirits, start praising God!

23. Instead of going to the extreme to make yourself attractive for people, put the same amount of energy into making yourself attractive to God. Praise Him!

CHAPTER 4
True Love

*L*ove is the most powerful principle in the Universe. Its true make up consists of everything that nourishes the soul and makes broken people whole. Satan also knows how powerful love is and how devastating it can be to his kingdom, and so he has done a good job of robbing people of the understanding of what love truly is. Everybody seeks it but don't really understand the true meaning of it.

When you don't understand what love is, you are incapable of giving it, and in a lot of cases even receiving it. The Bible says in 1 John 4:8 that God is love, so God Himself is the embodiment of what love is. This chapter's intent is to help us understand what love truly is and help us to identify true love from false love by understanding what love does.

What Love Is

1. The results that love yields is worth what it cost to give.

2. God is the total embodiment of what love is.

3. As powerful as God is, He doesn't force us to serve Him. He gives all of us the freedom to choose.

4. Sometimes a simple hello, smile, hug or handshake can be life-changing.

5. Nothing can compare, in all creation, to human beings. God created us like Him.

6. Because God's justice is perfect, His love also consists of His wrath.

7. Jesus was slaughtered because of our wrongs.

8. God's love is greater than any of our mistakes.

9. Love is what put Jesus on the cross, not the Jews.

10. Understanding what true love is only comes from knowing the One that is love.

11. True love is sacrificial.

12. True love is appreciative.

13. There is no greater demonstration of love than at the cross of Jesus Christ.

14. If you don't know what love does, you don't truly know what love is.

15. God is love, so love is God.

16. Jesus was convicted and killed for the crimes we committed.

17. No matter what happens when the sun sets, love is love.

18. We are always on God's mind. He thinks about us all the time continually.

19. People seek and get caught up in ungodly lifestyles due to a lack of understanding about the love of God. God's love is all we need.

20. There is absolutely nothing more satisfying than to know God's love.

21. One of the main reasons people are suicidal is because of a lack of understanding of God's unfailing love for them.

22. True love builds unbreakable bonds.

23. Through all the hills and valleys in life, God will be right there with you to see you through.

24. God's love makes everybody lovable.

25. Just like the chicken came before the egg, true love comes from genuine faith.

26. God's love is the answer concerning all of our struggles and mysteries that occur in our lives.

27. It was love that caused a righteous man to die for unrighteous people so we could follow Him before we even *decided* to follow Him. We love Him because He loved us first.

28. God's love can't be matched. No one can love you like the Lord.

29. When we receive Jesus as Savior and Lord, God gives us His love to love others through the Holy Spirit.

30. God showed us the immeasurable love He has for the whole world by sending His Son to die for people that didn't love Him.

31. Love brought death to an innocent Man, and as a result, that same love brought life to a multitude of guilty people.

32. As much as we have and continue to mess up, we still wake up every day to God's mercy and because of God's mercy.

33. God's grace is a combination of God's love and His mercy.

34. God, Himself, represents everything that love is.

35. God gave all He had and is still giving all He has, demonstrating a love that can't be matched.

36. Without God's love, nothing good would exist.

37. Although we use hearts as symbols of love, the cross is the world's greatest love symbol.

38. Everything that is good is tied to love.

39. We identify with Christ when we love each other.

40. God's love enables His children to love everyone, because His love is supernaturally working through His children.

41. God's love can carry us through anything.

42. God loves you, there is no question about that, But the question is, do you love God?

43. Love is contagious.

44. Truly knowing God begins with an experience that reveals His love for you.

45. Love God first, then God gives us knowledge, strength, and guidance to raise our kids.

46. Peace is a product of love.

47. Humility is a characteristic of love.

What Love Does

1. Lord, help me to treat others as you treat me.

2. It's hard sometimes to love people that don't have a true understanding of what love is, however, we must continue to love them understanding that love then begins to take on different faces.

3. Knowing what love does gives a clearer picture of what love is.

4. We are commanded to love everyone. However, *you have to feed some people with a long handle spoon.* (Words from Mrs. Lizzie Gates)

5. Even though God is concerned when we mess up, He is more interested in us repenting and continuing to move forward in Christ.

6. They say money makes the world go around, but really loves does.

7. If you truly love God, you will follow Him. If you don't truly love God, you won't. If you truly want to love God, you eventually will. But if you truly don't care about loving God, you never will.

8. Religion brings bondage to people, but Jesus sets people free.

9. One of the many amazing things about God is that He loves every single person ever born as

intimately as if we all were the only person ever born.

10. Jesus died to give us the privilege to pray. Don't ever take prayer for granted.

11. God's love offers grace and mercy to people that don't deserve it.

12. True love produces friendships and solid relationships.

13. True love breeds more of itself.

14. True love can be identified by what it does.

15. Love tells you the truth as opposed to catering to your feelings.

16. Observe what people say so you know how to minister to them effectively.

17. True love doesn't always feel good. It provides what is needed not necessarily what is wanted.

18. God's love is extended to everybody. No conditions.

19. Loving God compels you to love all kinds of people.

20. True love never turns a blind eye to justice.

21. Love is the most powerful principle that exists. It is love that rights wrongs, establishes peace, and heals broken relationships.

22. True love is compelled to tell people the truth, no matter what it may cost.

23. Lies and deception breed death, but true love breeds life.

24. The entire will of God is accomplished by truly loving God.

25. Sometimes love is not doing (or what you didn't do). It doesn't give in to the flesh.

26. It's impossible for a person that truly loves God to not genuinely love people.

27. True love chooses God's way of doing things as opposed to following their feelings.

28. Love can also be aggressive. The difference in love's aggression is that it's intent and timing is right.

29. Just as bread is nourishment for the body, so is love nourishment for our souls.

30. Love breeds faith and faith needs love to continue.

31. Doing what is right is challenging sometimes, but loving God more than what is challenging you compels you to do right.

32. True love forgives.

33. True love heals brokenness.

34. The face of God is revealed to unbelievers when believers love one another.

35. Sometimes some types of love put our hearts at risk, but never let that situation cause you to stop loving.

36. True love does more walking than talking.

37. If you love me, tell the truth, but if you love yourself more, don't.

38. Sometimes loving a person is keeping your distance from them.

39. The conviction of God is the love of God.

40. Pride will say it's not my fault, but love will compel you to apologize.

41. Love forgives every transgression, no matter what they are.

42. Forgiveness is a characteristic of love.

43. God's love will give you the wisdom and strength to make those hard decisions that have to be made in order for your child to grow into their proper Christ-like mold.

44. Conviction is something we all avoid. We hate how it feels, yet in reality, it alone is a redeeming minister second to none.

45. Sometimes love has to be stern.

46. Love elevates and/or restores.

This Isn't Love

1. Anything in our lives not connected to love is destructive.

2. People that aren't or feel they aren't loved usually live destructively.

3. Selfishness is love's number one enemy.

4. To stop loving is to stop living.

5. We chase people, who's love is faulty at best, and shun God, whose love is immeasurable.

6. Love is powerful. This is why evil people fabricate it to prey on the hearts of others.

7. Some of what we consider to be love is really harmful tolerance.

CHAPTER 5
Purpose

*G*od is both the Source and Creator of life. It's revolutionary to understand and believe these things, and that God has a specific role for each one of us to walk out. This is true concerning every human being no matter the circumstances from which you were born. In other words, God created all of us with a specific purpose in mind to live out. Living out this purpose brings us the ultimate fulfillment in life.

Remember, God is the Source of life and as Creator, He determines what that purpose is for each one of us. Seek Him diligently to discover what your purpose is and He will reveal it.

Walking in Purpose

1. When God-given talent lines up with God's call, the two working together produces instant and lasting results.

2. Some people in different relationships are called to places of suffering in order to be there to pick up the pieces and put things back together when the other party or parties fall.

3. The skills that people have are for more purposes than they may realize.

4. No matter what your background is or even your circumstances, God is able to bring your purpose to pass. Submit to Him, trust Him, and obey Him.

5. When people operate in purpose, lives are greatly affected and even changed.

6. God is glorified when we walk in purpose. God gave everyone an individual purpose which is unique, but it ties to the purpose that we all share in common.

8. Victory is attached to my name when I know my purpose and walk in it.

9. The purpose is knowing God's will for your life and doing it.

10. Your relationship with God is key to walking out your purpose.

11. Our common purpose as God's children is to preach the gospel to the lost. This can only be successfully accomplished by the Holy Spirit working through us.

12. Knowing what your purpose is, is life changing. You will never forget that moment when it is discovered.

13. As immediate as change comes when a light is turned on in a dark room, so it is with us when we discover our purpose.

14. Knowing your purpose assures that you are valuable and you have great worth.

15. There is a part of purpose that everyone shares in common and that is to tell everyone about Jesus and how He saves.

16. There is a confidence that is contagious in a person that knows who they are.

17. God's purpose for you is exciting. It is filled with supernatural events.

18. Even though we have an individual purpose, it takes us working together with many others to accomplish it.

19. Accomplishing purpose is challenging, but it is worth it.

20. Purpose is always connected to some type of ministry.

21. At the end of the day, purpose is about building God's kingdom.

22. Knowing your purpose is more fulfilling than any amount of riches.

22. No matter how great or insignificant people may be in the eyes of others, everyone that knows and walks in their purpose is great.

23. What really happens when you truly make up your mind to do something is that you've came to the end of yourself, allowing God to have control in the situation. Accomplishing purpose is then in effect.

24. How amazing it is to know that God created me with a plan for my life.

The Process

1. Destiny starts, continues, and is accomplished through a made up mind. There's power in a made up mind.

2. Not only have you been able to overcome many life-threatening hardships because of God's grace, but also because of God's purpose for your life. You're still here for a reason.

3. Accomplishing purpose will be accompanied with hardships and they are an essential part of the process. Be encouraged, don't quit.

4. Understand that it takes a process for accomplishments to be achieved. This brings encouragement during the rough times.

5. Our entire purpose is revealed to us by walking out the Great Commission.

6. Jesus needed Judas in order for God's plan to ultimately come to fruition, that's why He didn't rebuke him or kick him off the squad.

7. The truth sets people free, therefore, the bearer of it is not your enemy.

8. When dealing with heartbreak, the truth provides the solution. And although it might not immediately take the pain away, it will take it away in due time and turn your pain into strength. Accept the truth, be patient, and walk out the process.

9. The very reason for your existence is to accomplish your purpose. God created you for it.

10. People of vision are also people of great passion.

11. Believers have been given the keys to the kingdom. We must use them in order to accomplish our assignment.

12. Believe what God said concerning you and be obedient, and your purpose will come into fruition.

13. In order to walk out what God said about you, it requires a continual renewing of your mind.

14. Only the creator of a thing knows why it was created. And so, your true purpose can only be revealed by God.

15. If Satan can't stop you from receiving Jesus as Lord and Savior, his next goal is to keep you from understanding your purpose.

16. Even if you are saved and know what your purpose is, the next crucial principle that must be maintained is staying focused.

17. Truth is revealed when you're in God's presence and that truth is direction in pursuing your purpose.

18. God uses people to do His will in the earth. He connects us to certain people for certain seasons to take us to next levels in our purpose.

19. Everything that is positive stems from love. This is what purpose is for.

20. In Christ, as a part of the body of Christ, God created each one of us and equipped us with resources such as talents, gifts, and even our personalities to enable us to fulfill our purpose.

21. Accomplishing purpose requires relentlessness *and* living purpose on purpose.

22. God's favor is also key in accomplishing purpose.Telling people the truth and being merciful compels it.

23. The Holy Spirit reveals, empowers, and sustains us in our quest to accomplish purpose. In other words, our relationship with Him must be strong in order to be successful.

24. When God reveals purpose, He reveals the outcome but He expects us to walk out the process by faith.

25. Another important element in fulfilling purpose is to truly have unwavering faith in what your purpose is, so when obstacles occur, we don't give up, or when God opens unfamiliar doors, we recognize that it is Him.

26. Sometimes trials hit so hard that it feels like God is not there. At those times, you have to stand on whatever God said concerning you and your purpose in the first place.

27. When you are walking in purpose, as long as you stand, you will prevail no matter how tough the opposition is.

28. Some trials that we go through are necessary. They are training you for purpose.

29. We are not even in position to walk out purpose until we are born again.

30. Knowing what you were born to do makes going through trials a little easier.

31. Loving people and telling them about Jesus puts you on course with purpose.

32. Difficulty doesn't give you the green light to abort the mission.

33. In order to reach our God-given destiny, the Holy Spirit has to become our best friend.

34. Purpose is about taking care of God's business; the reward is Him taking care of yours.

35. The more obstacles you have to overcome, the more glory God receives.

36. Once you know your purpose, the enemy works overtime to try and make you doubt it.

37. Be careful who you share certain details with concerning your purpose, not everyone will understand or want to see you prosper.

The Reason We Exist

1. One major part of accomplishing purpose is to live by faith.

2. Jesus didn't come to die only. He also came to demonstrate how the kingdom of God works on earth, so we could carry on where He left off.

3. Great things happen when we use our God-given talent.

4. Every single day of our lives was already known by God before we were born.

5. God made all of us unique on purpose *for* purpose.

6. We are born to live out the purpose that God already had foreseen and made provision for.

7. You're not here by chance. God, your Designer and Creator, created you with a certain purpose in mind. It's up to you to pursue what it is.

8. As powerful as God is, He does what He does in the earth through chosen men. (This is why it's crucial to know our purpose.)

9. You're not here just to get money by any means, but rather to honor God according to the calling He created you to accomplish.

10. Destiny, and everything needed to accomplish it, is found in Christ.

11. Knowing purpose drives you to be an overcomer.

12. At the end of the day, your purpose being fulfilled changed lives and led souls to being saved.

13. Fulfilling our calling is not about us but for others to be blessed, enlightened, healed, delivered, and saved.

14. Even the unrighteous have purpose in God's overall plan.

15. God started preparing you for purpose before you were even aware you had one.

16. Another reason it's so important for you to know what your purpose is, is because your purpose includes your happiness, somebody else's encouragement, somebody else's needed mercy, somebody else's deliverance, and somebody else's blessing. Purpose is way bigger than just you.

17. Life, as it relates to purpose, is like a movie. God is the writer and director; we are the actors. All of us have a role to play in this movie called *Life*—a role that will build God's kingdom, bless and prosper others, and ourselves as well.

Not Knowing Is Fatal

1. When you begin to believe the wrong things about your identity, you then begin to speak them and eventually become them.

2. The truth is, your true identity is who God said you are.

3. Another major barricade to finding purpose is being consumed with fitting in.

4. If you are consumed with fitting in, you are more likely to develop a false identity of yourself.

5. Trials, tribulations, environment, skin color nor any other situation we experience in life defines us. God defines us, so seek Him to find out who you really are.

6. One of the top enemies of purpose is fear.

7. True self-worth is a huge component in being successful in accomplishing purpose.

8. Before that real encounter with God, all of us have a little Gideon in us. True purpose can only be revealed by the One who made us.

9. So many people are living apart from purpose thinking that a false identity is who they really are. Therefore, many people need to discover what purpose isn't before they can truly understand what it is.

10. God is totally precise and perfectly detailed in everything He does. This also holds true for your destiny and purpose. Seek Him diligently so you know what He's called you to do.

11. Purpose is ready to be discovered and blossom after truly knowing that God loves you.

12. Chasing money and status are serious purpose killers.

13. Following our own desires leads us to destruction, but submitting to God leads us to discovering and accomplishing purpose.

14. Our faith must also be solid concerning the fact that we are created in God's image, and the fact that He created us for a specific reason.

15. Living life outside of God's purpose is wasted time.

16. Even if a person discovers their purpose, if they choose not to use it for the Lord, at the end of the day, their lives are still fruitless.

17. Our purpose is precious to God; He doesn't delight in us not knowing it.

18. There's a lot riding on your purpose.

19. Knowledge of purpose and suicide can't coexist.

20. When we are walking out our purpose, we give
    hope to others.

CHAPTER 6
Walking Upright Before the Lord

*T*he Bible teaches believers according to Ephesians 5:1 to be imitators of God. This is a call for believers to live holy. Holy simply means to live set apart for God's purpose. "Walking Upright Before the Lord" consists of proverbs or short sayings that convey the will of God concerning Godly living. In order to please God, we have to know His will and character and live accordingly.

Staying Connected with God

1. Lord, help me to treat others the way you treat me.

2. Beware of racism. It is designed by Satan and has the potential to destroy entire ethnicities.

3. Race issues seem to instantly produce hostility. This is evidence that it is not of God.

4. Anything that takes control of you with much power and influence is a spirit.

5. At a glance, although being steadfast and being stubborn are a lot alike, don't confuse one for the other because being steadfast is rooted in God's righteousness, but stubbornness is rooted in self.

6. We tend to be willing to compromise many things, but what are we willing to compromise for righteousness sake?

7. Every single day presents a new opportunity to do whatever is required to draw closer to God. This should be where our primary focus is.

8. Ask the Lord for what you need and trust Him. He is the Lord Almighty.

9. Just because some men choose to misuse the gifts of the spirit doesn't mean the gifts themselves aren't real.

10. It's not feasible to expect to follow Christ without having the mind of Christ.

11. A person of prudence knows how to choose the most important thing from among many other choices.

12. Sincere giving is the key to unlock blessing's door.

13. God actually doesn't see all sins the same, but all sin is punishable with the same penalty.

14. Real representatives of Christ are life-changers by just being themselves.

15. Doing what's right is not always easy, but it is wise.

16. In order to grow, we must be willing to embrace what is right and then be willing to change.

17. God is always ready and willing to forgive us as long as we are willing to confess our wrongdoing and truly repent of it.

18. Because Jesus was a man, He truly understands our trials and struggles.

19. No matter who listens or who doesn't, believers are called to preach the gospel.

20. Everybody is listening to somebody's voice, the wise will listen to God.

21. When all is said and done, the condition of my soul is what matters.

22. Even when we don't understand why God requires certain things from us, whatever He says is always for our benefit. Be obedient.

23. The example of kingdom-living and the spreading of God's kingdom on earth is our responsibility. Share the gospel of Jesus Christ with every human being.

24. In addition to being born again, our minds must constantly be renewed in order to walk upright before the Lord.

25. Although the Bible tells us to confront our brothers who have fallen, if we do it with ulterior motives, we are judging them.

26. When it comes to people committing sins, the bottom line reason is selfishness.

27. God can't forgive you if you don't repent and ask Him to. Confess your sins to the Lord.

28. Just like we have to exercise to stay fit physically, we also have to exercise by meditating on God's word to stay fit spiritually.

29. True freedom only comes through Christ Jesus.

30. Our mission as believers is to demonstrate how heaven operates on earth.

31. Holy living keeps us connected with the Lord.

32. The discovery and application of truth is the only way to truly be free.

33. True repentance only comes from a broken spirit.

34. It's bad when we become so comfortable with sin that we become immune to the truth.

35. God demands all of your allegiance.

36. Believing in God is not the same as trusting in God.

37. Righteousness can be painful and seem destructive initially, but in the end, it pays off.

38. Some of our blessings are being held back in certain areas because we refuse to let go of certain things and allow God to change our blessing-blocking perspective on these matters.

39. Those who have an ear will obtain the truth, or take in the truth and go out and do it.

40. God reveals mysteries through prayer.

41. Never make decisions based upon how you feel. Connect with the architect of the ages so you will see the big picture first, which will enable you to know where you're headed during the process.

42. Whatever you do and whatever you say is spirituality equivalent to a person physically planting a seed in the ground. And one day those seeds will produce a crop of whatever you planted.

43. We serve God by serving people.

44. It's time for us to trust God and cancel the media buzz.

45. God reveals secrets and mysteries in prayer.

46. Prejudice doesn't reflect the Father in any shape or form.

47. Racism can be so subtle that you don't even know it's there until certain situations occur and brings it out.

48. Your flesh has to be dealt with every day. And when you're in the midst of a storm, the battle is intensified two to three times over.

49. In the past, God winked at the wrong man did, but now commands all men to repent and become His.

50. The enemy wants us to just react and not think, but God wants us to trust Him and obey.

51. If we would put Christ first in our lives, everything else would fall into place.

52. Jesus is our lifeline, therefore, we must remain connected to Him in order to live.

53. Don't allow offenses to rob you of or limit your relationship with God.

54. Jesus was born to die, so that in Him we then could die to live.

55. Jesus Himself was redemption in the flesh.

56. God's ways establish a solid foundation for our lives and without that foundation somewhere down the line our lives crumble.

57. There is a difference in hearing the Word and receiving it.

58. Choose to follow Jesus and avoid getting caught up in the "monkey see, monkey do" syndrome.

59. Live by what is written, not by what we feel.

60. Sometimes God uses our issues to get our attention.

61. You never know how much being obedient to God in simple things is affecting others.

62. When we take credit for what God has done, we then take God out of the equation and disconnect ourselves from our very life source.

63. When we acknowledge our sins, God is ready and willing to forgive us.

64. The enemy will have you believing that crap is a delicacy, but the Lord is a God of truth.

65. Unholy living gives the enemy full access into your life to wreak havoc.

66. Realizing that we are not living just to please ourselves is a game changer.

67. God sacrificed His Son, and put His Spirit in us so we could live holy.

68. If we're going to live a life that pleases God, His will has to be more important to us than anything else.

69. Don't worry, follow Jesus.

70. Don't do you, do Jesus.

71. The narrow road may not be the easiest to travel, but in the end, it's payoff has eternal value.

72. A lot of people consider themselves to be in good standing with God because they're good people, yet Jesus said nobody is good except God.

73. Holiness brings freedom.

74. You can't live according to your own desires and expect God's approval.

Spiritual Warfare

1. Prayer cannot be contained by time or place. Its power exceeds both.

2. Where truth (God's word) doesn't reside, there is bondage to take its place.

3. Condemnation puts you in chains, conviction sets you free from chains.

4. A strong enough connection with God seats us in the heavenlies.

5. The devil's number one weapon against us is deception. Our counter is the truth which is the Word of God.

6. The armor of God is not meant to be put on, taken off, and put back on again repeatedly, but rather put on and left on while continually growing in how to use it.

7. The enemy hides himself (his presence, his tactics) in filth (physically and spiritually speaking). Cleanliness (physically and spiritually speaking) exposes him and his devices.

8. There is a spirit that causes people to do the opposite of what they should. The effects of it are called the reverse effect.

9. If we will trust God through turmoil, we will find that His word is true.

10. Suffering comes with the territory of being a Christian—some to more degrees than others.

11. Suffering for the kingdom doesn't always mean your walk isn't right.

12. God has given His people authority to set His standards in the earth.

13. Refusing to humble yourself before the Lord only keeps you trapped in a boxing match with yourself.

14. If we are willing to take an unwavering stand for God, He will fight for us.

15. Shunning God is to partner with the enemy.

16. Fold your arms on the devil, letting him know you're done falling for and giving in to his plots and schemes.

17. Satan is a freeloader; He's not leaving unless you kick him out.

18. One word the enemy loves to hear is *well.*

19. Some people think that shunning God is beneficial, but in reality, it is the total opposite.

20. We must become skilled swordsmen to defeat the enemy.

21. Spiritual warfare is continuous in the lives of God's people, and if we don't fight, we definitely won't win.

22. The devil doesn't attack you with physical weapons, neither can you fight or defeat him with guns and knives.

23. When you make up your mind to do anything God's way, expect the enemy to attack. Stand firm.

24. When the war is on, decide to follow Christ as opposed to your feelings.

25. Spiritual warfare is ongoing, so stay dressed for the occasion. Keep your armor on.

CHAPTER 7
God Is Our Everything

*W*e serve a God that has no beginning and has no end. He is all-powerful, ever-present, and all-knowing. He created the heavens, the earth, and everything in them, yet the Bible declares that out of everything God created, human beings are second only to the angels. However, we are still God's most adored creation.

He created us in His own image and when we fell, He sent His only Son to die as a sacrifice for our redemption, restoring the relationship between man and Himself. He loves us unconditionally, and His grace and mercy are everlasting. All that we have and all that we can become is because of Him. He is our everything!

God Almighty

1. The Bible is God's diary. It contains what He thinks and how He feels about everything.

2. God's diary reveals His heart, so we can truly know Him.

3. Everything God has for us starts and ends with Jesus Christ.

4. Whether we love God or hate Him, whether we believe in Jesus or worship Satan, we all need the Lord!

5. All believers must develop a relationship with God through the Holy Spirit. He and He only guides and empowers us to complete God's will perfectly.

6. In all situations in life, seek the Lord and His will, trust what He tells you and do it. This is the true meaning of good success.

7. To serve God half-heartedly is to not serve Him at all.

8. In order to go to heaven, you must first die.

9. When we transition from loving God for what He does to loving God because of who He is, knowing God goes to another level.

10. There is no greater comfort than knowing we are truly children of God.

11. It is completely feasible to trust in a perfect and almighty God. We just have to be willing.

12. God knew every detail about your life before you were born. He is eternal and all-knowing.

13. Wherever God's people meet together in The House of Prayer or The Meeting Place, the purpose is to praise and worship God together, and God Himself meets us there and meets all of our needs.

14. God's forgiveness is so pure and powerful that it's as if you never did the thing you've been forgiven for.

15. Hope in Christ is perfect security.

16. Only Jesus can bridge the gap between God and man.

17. Because Jesus was both God and man, He was able to experience what we go through and respond perfectly, giving us the perfect model of what a Christian's life is supposed to look like.

18. As long as God's children realize who He is to them, nothing is impossible.

19. The majesty of God exceeds our ability to comprehend or imagine.

20. God exists on His own, never having a beginning or an end.

21. Every single thing we will ever need has already been stored up for us in heavenly places.

22. God's dealings with men come only through covenants.

23. Jesus (being God) wears many hats. The more we know about the many roles that Jesus has, the better we know God through Him.

24. In the midst of trials, trust God as opposed to reacting based on our feelings.

25. God Himself and God alone is perfect. Our minds having never experienced what true perfection is like can't even fathom what it is.

26. Sometimes life can throw curve balls, and it would appear that some situations are hopeless. But there is no situation that could occur in your life that God can't fix.

27. Jesus is the Lord of the lives of those who truly believe in God.

28. Only Jesus, through His blood, can rid people of their sins.

29. If you're tired, humble yourself before the Lord, who is able to change and sustain you.

30. Stop living according to your feelings. Trust and depend on an all-powerful God.

31. God has never failed and He never will.

32. Just because things don't happen when you think they should, doesn't mean that they won't. God is able.

33. In the fullness of time, God moves and makes things happen.

34. The heavens and the earth and all that is in them match the fingerprints of God.

35. There isn't any situation that could ever occur in anyone's life that God isn't able to fix.

36. With God, there is no such thing as impossible.

37. Miracles are normal to God.

38. Christ is Sovereign so we should rep Him relentlessly as such.

39. God is the Creator of heaven and earth and everything within the perimeters of the two.

40. The Lord sees and knows all. He knew the end even before there was a beginning.

41. The cross of Jesus Christ is the eternal crutch for man's fall.

42. Even as a baby, Jesus had King Herod restless.

43. Jesus was killed for sin by sinners, while asking the Father to forgive them.

44. When counseling people, the Holy Spirit must do the solving, directing, and talking.

45. Sheep connected to the Shepherd have the power to kill giants.

46. Jesus took a beating for our healing and hung naked to rid us of our shame. Now all power and authority are in His name.

47. There aren't any impossibilities to those who remain in Christ.

48. The breath we breathe is the same breath God blew into the nostrils of Adam. God is the giver of life.

49. Jesus Christ is the true treasure my heart yearns for.

50. Life without Christ is living second rate by choice.

51. In creation, God spoke and the Holy Spirit manifested what He spoke. It's the Spirit of God that performs what the Father says.

52. We can choose to live however we want and believe whatever we choose to believe, but regardless, God is still sovereign and reigns supreme. God is God no matter what!

53. Christ enables us to endure whatever comes our way in life, so there aren't any obstacles that can stop us.

54. We serve a God that gives us commandments in areas that others only can recommend or suggest, because He and He alone is sovereign.

55. If we choose to not accept Jesus as Savior and Lord, we choose not to be the original that He created you to be. We forfeit the value that God created us for by choice.

56. Although we can forfeit our value and worth by our own choices, every person (no matter who they are or what their lifestyle consists of), in the grand scheme of things, is totally valuable simply because God created us.

57. No man or any other being will ever come close to matching our God.

58. Hell is the absence of the love of God.

59. The Lord our God is perfect, therefore, He is totally trustworthy.

60. It's not the what, it's the why. Having to see God or else, is the what; but believing in Him despite not seeing Him, is the why.

61. God meant what He said in His word. It's nonnegotiable.

62. It is unwise to resist, rebuke, or reprove anything that falls within the perimeters of God's will.

63. God is perfect and He operates from that perspective and realm.

64. Jesus is the only person ever to have once been a spirit, and then became a full-blooded human being.

65. Who else but God just is.? Who else is there that exist on their own?

66. God is always working, even when it seems like nothing is going on.

67. God invested everything He had in us, that being His only begotten Son.

The Word of God

1. Whatever God says in His word is for our betterment. God is already perfect, lacking nothing.

2. God and the words written in the Bible are one in the same. In the beginning, the Word was with God and the Word was God (John 1:1).

3. Every single thing that exists will one day perish. The only thing that will never perish is the Word of God.

4. The Word of God reveals His ways. This is how we get to know Him.

5. The only thing that can save a person's soul is the message of the Gospel of Jesus Christ.

6. Hearing and doing what the Word of God says can make weak people strong and ignorant people wise.

7. The Word of God is an enemy to those who oppose God and/or His righteousness.

8. Truth and Jesus are synonymous with one another.

9. The source of truth, which is God, is the truth.

10. The Word of God is all we need in order to know how to live right.

11. God is the source of true wisdom.

12. The Word of God has the ability to meet ALL of our needs.

13. The Word of God is the only thing on earth that is eternal in and of itself.

14. The origin of life itself came from what God said.

15. God's word is more powerful than nuclear weapons.

16. God's word teaches and rebukes.

17. God's word establishes kings.

18. God's word sets things in motion and makes things happen.

19. God's word can manifest miracles.

20. The Word of God is alive because the Word is Jesus Himself. This means that every word God spoke has never-ending wisdom and life-changing power.

21. When your heart is hard, it is impossible to receive the Word of God.

22. If you dance with fear, it will go home with you. Trust God's word concerning you—obey and be free.

23. A lot of people hear the Word of God and view it as knowledge but fail to view it as instructions.

24. God's word details instructions for our whole lives.

25. The Bible says a lot more than it actually says.

26. The Word of God is God; therefore, everything God is, His word is also.

27. If we live by the Word, we will live.

28. If you don't believe what Jesus said, you don't believe in Him.

29. In order to imitate Christ, we must first know Him.

30. Judas was one of Jesus' original 12 disciples, yet he chose not to know Him.

31. God's word never perishes; it is eternal and true.

32. As God's children, we have lots of promises to lay claim to.

33. God has never made a mistake, nor acted outside of His own rules.

Epilogue

Decision-making is crucial because it directly affects the outcome of our lives. I can remember when I was younger finding myself in situations I didn't want to be in. After sitting down and analyzing how I got there, more times than not, it was traced back to hasty, selfish, or just plain foolish decisions I had made. I then began to understand that I had to go back to something that was instilled in me as a little boy, and that was establishing principles and making decisions based on them.

I believe the proverbs I've included under each principle will enhance your decision-making and be a blessing to you. If you are dedicated to following them, I've grown to learn that having the right principles will bring you through even the toughest situations in life. Faith, wisdom, praise, love, purpose, living holy, and recognizing that without God we're nothing, are all principles that we can base our day-to-day decision-making on, and know that they are the right decisions to make.

About the Author

Stephen Perry is the founder of Fire by Night Tabernacle Ministry where he has pastored a small congregation for 10 years and has been an active Bible study teacher and head of The Street Tour outreach ministry.

Beyond the church walls, he is the CEO of Liite Slanga Productions record label, holding the positions of head engineer, producer and artist. He is also the owner and grill master at Da Liite House Southern Barbecue, and is now adding published author to his growing list of accomplishments.

The proverbs shared in this book were obtained mainly from the many trials Stephen has been through, coupled with wisdom that God spoke to him in the midst of those situations. From birth, God's grace has been super active in his life to this very moment, and he is grateful to have yet another platform to share the goodness of God as it relates to all that He has done for and through him. Stephen is the husband of Christina Perry, father of six children, and resides in Phoenix, Arizona.